BAPTISM
Who Needs It?

ROBERT J. BARNETT

REGULAR BAPTIST
RBP Press

Robert J. Barnett, a pastor,
was converted while serving in the
U. S. Marine Corps.

Dedication
With deep love and thanksgiving
for my wife, Debby, whose steadfast
love and childlike faith have been
an encouragement to me.

Cover design: Carol Swanson
Illustrations: T. L. Powell

Baptism—Who Needs It?
© 1991
Regular Baptist Press • Arlington Heights, Illinois
www.RegularBaptistPress.org • 1-800-727-4400

Printed in U.S.A.
All rights reserved

RBP5203 • ISBN: 978-0-87227-171-5
2017 Printing

"Then they that gladly received his word were baptized" (Acts 2:41).

C hristians should be keenly aware of the basic ingredients of the Christian life and how to use them. In Acts 2 we see the ingredients in the lives of the first church. There is a flow pattern to follow.

DISCIPLESHIP FLOW

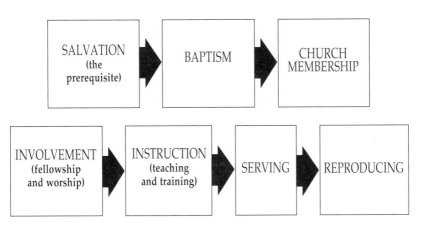

These studies have been developed to help you learn these truths in the context of a discipleship relationship. The memory verses will help you take the Word of God to heart.

Discovery is the key to these studies. You will discover for yourself the plan of God from the Bible. Only then will you be ready to decide what you need to do.

God Accepts You

At the moment you placed your faith in the Savior, the Lord Jesus Christ, you experienced the "new birth" and became a child of God!

"But as many as received him, to them gave he power [the right] to become the sons [children] of God, even to them that believe on his name" (John 1:12).

Acceptance with God

When Jesus died on the cross, *all* your sins were still in the future, weren't they?

His death paid the penalty for all your sins—
    all the sins in your past;
    all the sins you do today;
    all the sins in your future.

What are you as a Christian to do when you sin?

1 John 1:9 _____

Our confession is still accepted only on the basis of the sacrificial blood of Jesus. On the cross He declared, *"It is finished."*

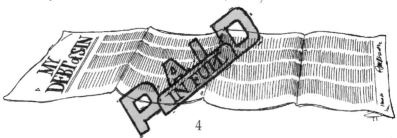

Review Questions

1. What is it that washed away your sin and released you from sin's penalty?

   Romans 3:25 _____

   _____

   Revelation 1:5 _____

   _____

2. Upon *whose* righteousness and life is your salvation based?

   Romans 5:10 _____

   Romans 5:17 _____

   2 Corinthians 5:20, 21 _____

   1 Peter 2:21–24 _____

It is extremely important for you as a growing Christian to know that your *acceptance* with God is based completely upon the blood of our Savior Jesus Christ, which He shed on the cross. Your *acceptance* is based on what *He alone* has done.

A Verse to Memorize

"Therefore being justified by faith, we have peace with God through our Lord Jesus Christ: by whom also we have access by faith into this grace wherein we stand" (Romans 5:1, 2).

2 ▶ Pleasing God

Accepted only because of **His** blood... and I can't add to it!

Then... why be baptized?

D o you know the difference between being accepted by God and your obedience to God, which is pleasing to Him? God has accepted you as His child, but He wants you to live a life that pleases Him. When we obey Him, He is pleased; but when we disobey Him, He is grieved. His desires for us are given in the Bible, our instruction book for living the Christian life.

- ACCEPTANCE with God is based on the blood of Jesus. I cannot add to His sacrifice.

- PLEASING God involves obeying God as His revelation, called the Bible, shows us how.

- BAPTISM does not have anything to do with my acceptance with God, but it is the first step God wants me to take in *pleasing* Him.

A Verse to Memorize
"And he commanded them to be baptized in the name of the Lord" (Acts 10:48).

Baptism Is Important

B aptism is important to our Savior, the Lord Jesus Christ. Jesus began His own ministry on earth by being baptized by John the Baptist in the Jordan River. One of the last things Jesus commanded His disciples to do was to baptize new converts.

Baptism Commanded by Christ

"And Jesus came and spake unto them, saying, All power is given unto me in heaven and in earth. Go ye therefore, and teach all nations, baptizing them in the name of the Father, and of the Son, and of the Holy Ghost" (Matthew 28:18, 19).

This command of our Lord applies to us today. Matthew 28:20 makes this fact clear.

Review Question

Is it God's desire that *you* be baptized? _____

The Early Church Practiced Baptism

The church began on the Day of Pentecost. This event is recorded in Acts 2. The practice of baptism was found universally in the New Testament church.

Review Questions

1. What was the first thing the new Christians were told to do following conversion?

   Acts 2:38 _____

   Note: "For" the forgiveness, or remission, of sins means "because of" the forgiveness of sins. In other words, baptism doesn't save us. It is an act of obedience after we have been saved.

2. What was the first thing the new believers did after receiving (believing) the Word?

Acts 2:41 _____

3. List each step the new believers followed in Acts 2:41 and 42.

(1) <u>Were Saved</u> (Believed His Word) (4) _____

(2) <u>Were Baptized</u> (5) _____

(3) _____ (6) _____

Read Acts 8:26–38.

4. What did the Ethiopian eunuch ask Philip?

Acts 8:36 _____

5. What did Philip answer?

Acts 8:37 _____

6. What did Philip the Evangelist then do?

Acts 8:38 _____

7. What did Peter do to the new believers he led to the Lord?

Acts 10:48 _____

Believer's baptism was practiced throughout the New Testament church. Do you believe God *desires* for you to be baptized?_____

• Commanded by Christ

• Practiced by the church

Baptism—What Does It Mean?

You have now seen that baptism has nothing to do with gaining acceptance with God and that it is very important to God that you be baptized. Let's look at what baptism means.

"I Pledge Allegiance"

Baptism is the first test of obedience that God gives a new Christian. It shows us whether or not we want to please Him. It is a pledge of allegiance to the Lord.

A Verse to Memorize

"Then they that gladly received his word were baptized" (Acts 2:41).

In baptism we take our stand with Jesus in front of other people and confess our faith and desire to please Him. It is our first step of *separation* from the world.

Do you desire to please the Lord, Who died for you? _____

9

Baptism Is a Picture

Baptism is a picture, or symbol, of what happens in salvation. It is *identification* with what Jesus did on the cross. It outwardly pictures an inward reality.

A Picture of the Gospel

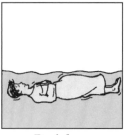

| Death | Burial | Resurrection |

1. We are baptized into His _____.
   (Romans 6:3)

2. We have been _____ with Him in baptism.
   (Romans 6:4)

3. We have been _____ with Him to walk in newness
   of life. (Romans 6:4, 5)

Paul used the symbol of baptism to show that when a person trusts in Christ for salvation, he or she is identified with the benefits of His death and resurrection. We as believers have died in respect to sin's power over us and have been empowered by God to live a new life that pleases Him.

A Verse to Memorize

"Therefore if any man be in Christ, he is a new creature: old things are passed away; behold, all things are become new" (2 Corinthians 5:17).

Who Is to Be Baptized?

A careful reading of the New Testament clearly demonstrates that Christian baptism is believer's baptism. It must *follow* salvation.

Believers Only

1. What was the prerequisite set forth to the Ethiopian eunuch?

   Acts 8:36–38 _____

   _____

2. What people were baptized on the Day of Pentecost?

   Acts 2:41 _____

In the command of Christ to baptize new disciples, it is clear that He was talking about those who had placed their faith in Jesus. All the examples of baptism in the New Testament are people old enough to understand the gospel and to place their faith personally and consciously in Christ. (Biblical examples include Lydia and her household. She was obviously either a widow or unmarried. Her "household" would refer to servants, not to infants or to children not yet accountable. The Philippian jailer is a similar case. Acts 16:34 indicates his household became believers before they were baptized.)

3. Who did Philip baptize?

   Acts 8:12 _____

Baptism signifies an identification with Christ and His completed work on the cross and can pertain only to those who have professed faith in Christ for salvation.

6 ► How Am I to Be Baptized?

T he New Testament church practiced immersion, which means to put the person being baptized completely under the water. In fact, the command to "baptize" is a command to immerse.

"Baptize" Means "Immerse"

Our English word "baptism" is a transliteration of the Greek word *baptizo*. In other words, the translators simply put English letters to the Greek sounds.

If you had lived in New Testament times and heard the word *baptizo,* you would have known that the speaker meant to dip, submerge, or immerse.

All the major Greek dictionaries (lexicons) tell us *baptizo* means "to immerse" or "to submerge." In fact, the word could be used to refer to a drowning, to the sinking of a ship, or even to the idea of perishing.

Every time the New Testament refers to the practice of baptism, it uses the word *baptizo*. If the writer wanted to allow pouring or sprinkling, he would have chosen other Greek words, but he did not. Neither did Jesus!

Biblical Examples of Immersion

In every example of the act of baptism, immersion is either implied or allowed for.

1. Describe the method of Jesus' baptism.

   Mark 1:9, 10 _____

2. Why did John the Baptist choose to baptize near Aenon?

   John 3:23 _____

3. The Ethiopian eunuch traveled in a caravan that certainly had an abundant supply of water that could have been used for sprinkling or pouring if either mode were baptism. But where did Philip baptize the eunuch?

Acts 8:36, 38 _____

4. How is his baptism described?

Acts 8:38 _____

Symbolism Demands Immersion

You have already learned that baptism not only demonstrates your loyalty to God, but it also pictures Christ's death, burial, and resurrection. Only immersion can do this.

5. Does the Bible teach a specific method for baptism?

_____

6. What method does the Bible teach? _____

- Meaning of the word

- Examples of baptism

- Symbolism of immersion

A Verse to Memorize

"If ye love me, keep my commandments" (words spoken by Jesus, John 14:15).

13

7 Apply It

Answer these questions about yourself.

1. What is the only reason God accepts me?

   _____

2. Does baptism help me be accepted by God? _____

   _____

3. Does God want *me* to be baptized? _____

4. Will I please Him if I refuse? _____

5. What does baptism mean to me? _____

   _____

   _____

6. Who is to be baptized? _____

7. Am I willing to pledge my allegiance to the Lord by
   being baptized by immersion as a believer? _____

   _____

If you are ready to be baptized, then tell the pastor or the person
helping you with these Bible studies. It will be their privilege to assist
you in following the Lord in believer's baptism.

> "Trust and obey—
> For there's no other way
> To be happy in Jesus
> But to trust and obey."

*You may want to remove the baptismal certificate
on the next page, fill it out, and frame it.*

My Christian Baptism

This certificate declares that as a result of believing on the Lord Jesus Christ as my personal Savior, I,

_____,

have followed my Lord's command and example and have been baptized in the name of the Father and the Son and the Holy Spirit. I have publicly proclaimed my identification with the Lord Jesus Christ's death, burial, and resurrection

on the_____ day of _____, 20____

at

_____

Church and Location

_____

Baptizing Pastor